FREEDOM'S PROMISE

HIDDEN
HEROES
THE HUMAN COMPUTERS OF NASA

BY DUCHESS HARRIS, JD, PHD

WITH REBECCA ROWELL

Core Library

An Imprint of Abdo Publishing
abdobooks.com

Cover image: Annie Easley did important calculations
as a human computer for NASA.

abdocorelibrary.com

Published by Abdo Publishing, a division of ABDO, PO Box 398166, Minneapolis, Minnesota 55439. Copyright © 2019 by Abdo Consulting Group, Inc. International copyrights reserved in all countries. No part of this book may be reproduced in any form without written permission from the publisher. Core Library™ is a trademark and logo of Abdo Publishing.

Printed in the United States of America, North Mankato, Minnesota
092018
012019

Cover Photo: NASA
Interior Photos: NASA, 1, 6–7, 10, 13, 16–17, 18, 32, 43; Duchess Harris, 5, 26–27; Felt & Tarrant Mfg Co/New–York tribune/Library of Congress, 21; Red Line Editorial, 23, 40; NASA/Interim Archives/Archive Photos/Getty Images, 29; Smith Collection/Gado/Archive Photos/Getty Images, 34–35; Bob Nye/NASA/Donaldson Collection/Michael Ochs Archives/Getty Images, 36

Editor: Maddie Spalding
Series Designer: Claire Vanden Branden

Library of Congress Control Number: 2018949708

Publisher's Cataloging-in-Publication Data

Names: Harris, Duchess, author. | Rowell, Rebecca, author.
Title: Hidden heroes: the human computers of NASA / by Duchess Harris and Rebecca Rowell.
Other title: The human computers of NASA
Description: Minneapolis, Minnesota : Abdo Publishing, 2019 | Series: Freedom's promise | Includes online resources and index.
Identifiers: ISBN 9781532117701 (lib. bdg.) | ISBN 9781641856041 (pbk) | ISBN 9781532170560 (ebook)
Subjects: LCSH: African American women mathematicians--Juvenile literature. | Aerospace engineers--United States--Juvenile literature. | United States National Aeronautics and Space Administration--Juvenile literature.
Classification: DDC 629.45--dc23

CONTENTS

A LETTER FROM DUCHESS 4

CHAPTER ONE
NASA's Secret Weapon 6

CHAPTER TWO
The Path to NASA 16

CHAPTER THREE
Working at NASA 26

CHAPTER FOUR
Trailblazers 34

Fast Facts 42

Stop and Think 44

Glossary 45

Online Resources 46

Learn More 46

About the Authors 47

Index 48

A LETTER FROM DUCHESS

My grandmother, Miriam Daniel Mann, was born in Covington, Georgia, on July 25, 1907. In 1943, she heard that NACA was looking to hire women to do calculations by hand. This was the National Advisory Committee for Aeronautics. NACA later became NASA. Many women, known as human computers, helped in the early US space program.

My mother's early memories are of her mother talking about doing math problems all day. Back then a lot of the math was done with a #2 pencil and the aid of a slide rule.

I was born two years after my grandmother passed, in 1969. That was the year that the United States landed on the moon. I was inspired by interviews with my mother from 2011, which is why I wrote this book. Our story is a story for everyone.

Join me in this journey to learn about the Hidden Heroes of NASA. Join me in a journey that tells the story of the promise of freedom.

Duchess Harris

Miriam Daniel Mann worked as a human computer at NASA for more than 20 years.

CHAPTER
ONE

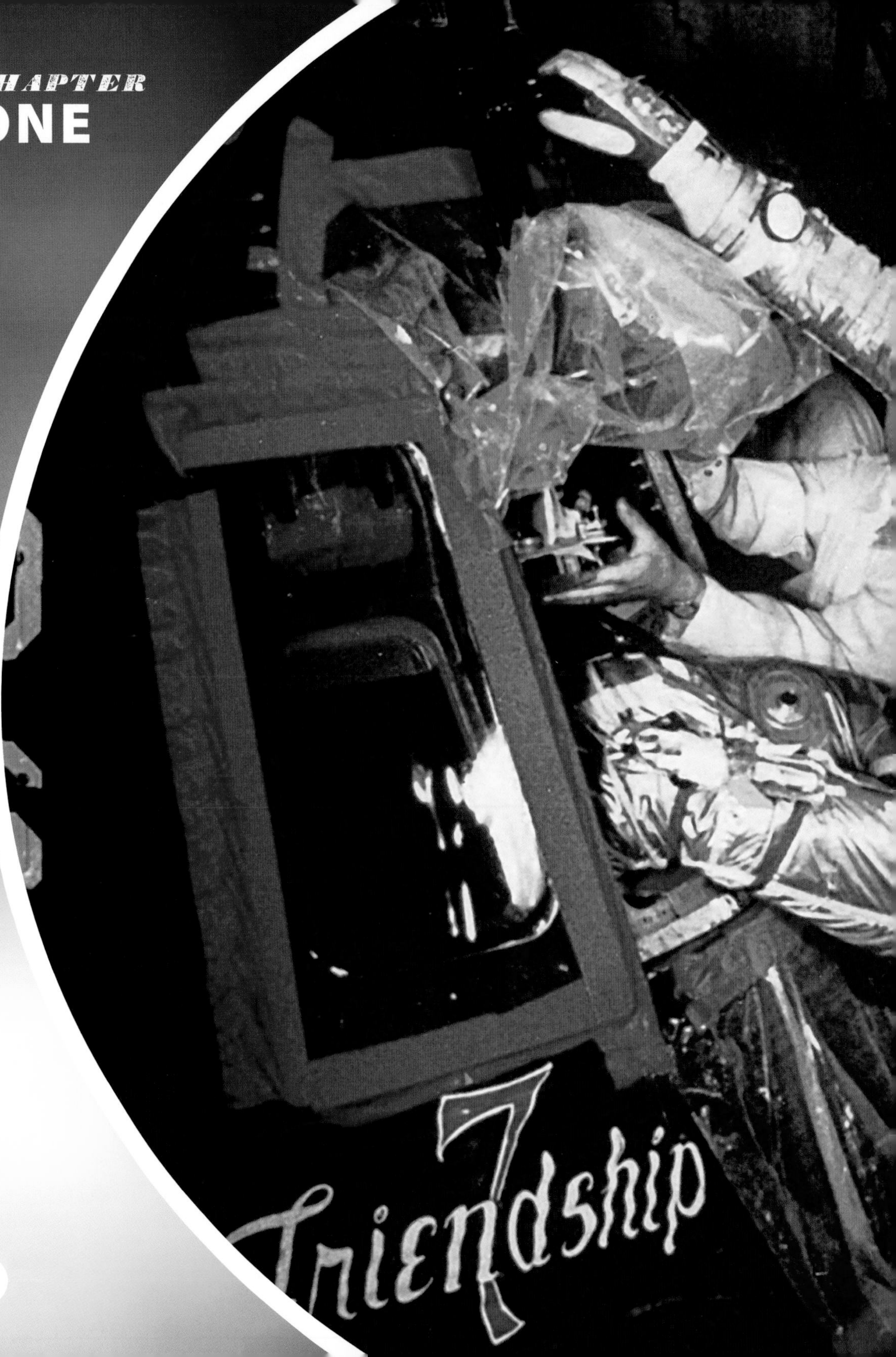

NASA'S SECRET WEAPON

I n the fall of 1961, astronaut John Glenn was preparing for his mission to orbit Earth. One of his preflight tasks was verifying where he would reenter Earth's atmosphere and land. This process required complicated mathematics. Glenn needed a mathematician with special skills. At the National Aeronautics and Space Administration (NASA), the people who did this math were called human computers.

The work of human computers helped make NASA astronaut John Glenn's mission to orbit Earth successful.

Glenn told one of his supervisors, "Get the girl to do it." The "girl" he was referring to was human computer Katherine Johnson. Glenn knew she was one of NASA's top mathematical minds.

The United States was fighting the Soviet Union to be the best in the world. A rivalry had emerged between the two countries after World War II (1939–1945). This rivalry was called the Cold War (1947–1991). The two superpowers were battling to outdo each other in every area. That included the new frontier of space exploration. Astronauts were making history and becoming heroes in a competition known as the space race.

Behind the scenes, people at NASA were working hard to make the United States the leader in the space race. NASA managed the US space program. Employees included engineers and scientists. Mathematicians worked at NASA too. Johnson was one of them.

THE NEED FOR COMPUTERS

Glenn's mission was important for science and technology. The mission was perhaps even more important because of the space race. The Soviet Union had already sent the first human into space earlier in the year. Soviet cosmonaut Yuri Gagarin orbited Earth once on April 12, 1961. NASA sent astronaut Alan Shepard into space on May 5, but he did not orbit the planet. That was Glenn's mission. Glenn needed to succeed

African American mathematician Melba Roy Mouton was the leader of a group of NASA human computers in the 1960s.

to match the Soviets' accomplishment. Failure was not an option.

NASA relied on human computers. They did the calculations that engineers, astronauts, and others relied on. NASA had an entire unit of women doing this important work. Many of them were white. Some, such as Johnson, were African American. Few people knew about Johnson and NASA's black women computers at the time and for decades after Glenn's flight. These women were NASA's hidden computers and secret weapon.

In the 1960s, computing was ready to move into the electronic age. NASA had recently started using an electronic computer. Workers had programmed equations into the computer that specified Glenn's orbit. The programming would control the path of *Friendship 7*, the capsule Glenn would ride in. But astronauts

OTHER SPACE WORK

Johnson worked on calculations for many different space projects. She calculated the trajectory for astronaut Alan Shepard's historic flight in May 1961. Shepard became the first American in space. The year before that, Johnson had written a report with engineer Ted Skopinski. In it, they provided the landing equations for a spacecraft orbiting Earth. Johnson was the first woman in NASA's Flight Research Division to receive credit for writing a report.

such as Glenn were not ready to trust machines to do the job. Glenn knew that he could rely on Johnson's calculations.

THE MISSION

Glenn would be the only astronaut on *Friendship 7*. Tensions were high. NASA wanted Glenn's capsule to land in a specific place in the Atlantic Ocean. If it struck land, he would die. If it approached Earth at the wrong angle, it would not be able to reenter the planet's atmosphere. The trajectory, or path, the capsule needed to follow was an arc.

Johnson did as Glenn asked. She checked the computer's work. She performed the same calculations using the same numbers. Johnson calculated where the capsule would be at any given time on the trajectory. The calculations were tricky. They took Johnson two weeks to do. But she had years of experience doing similar computations. Her calculations matched the

Katherine Johnson does calculations at NASA's Langley Research Center in 1962.

computer's calculations. Glenn got the confirmation he needed.

SUCCESS!

Glenn's launch had been canceled five times because of weather and equipment failures. Finally, on February 20, 1962, he boarded *Friendship 7* and launched into space. Glenn spent 4 hours, 55 minutes, and 23 seconds in space. Engineers and others at NASA worried Glenn and his capsule would burn up during reentry. Luckily, that did not happen. He orbited Earth three times before landing safely in the Atlantic Ocean.

Glenn's success that day was partly a result of Johnson's calculations. Many of the hidden computers were part of NASA before there was a space program and when the agency had a different name. Their work helped flight technology advance from aircraft to spacecraft. They helped create the US space program. Their work lived on after them, taking astronauts to the Moon and inspiring later generations.

STRAIGHT TO THE
SOURCE

Margot Lee Shetterly wrote a book about NASA's black women computers called *Hidden Figures*. In March 2014, Shetterly spoke at NASA's Langley Research Center for Women's History Month. She said:

> The reason these women are able to be in the positions they are . . . has very much to do with the female pioneers who came to NASA, and to its predecessor the NACA, back in the 1930s, the 1940s, through the 1950s and '60s. . . . This is a really strong example of how women rise to the occasion in a very high pressure scientific endeavor. All eyes [are] on this man as he's going into space and this is the woman [Katherine Johnson] who stood behind the man and checked the numbers.

Source: Joe Atkinson. "From Computers to Leaders: Women at NASA Langley." *NASA*. National Aeronautics and Space Administration, March 27, 2014. Web. Accessed May 29, 2018.

Consider Your Audience

Adapt this passage for a different audience, such as your teacher or friends. Write a blog post conveying this same information for the new audience. How does your post differ from the original text and why?

CHAPTER TWO

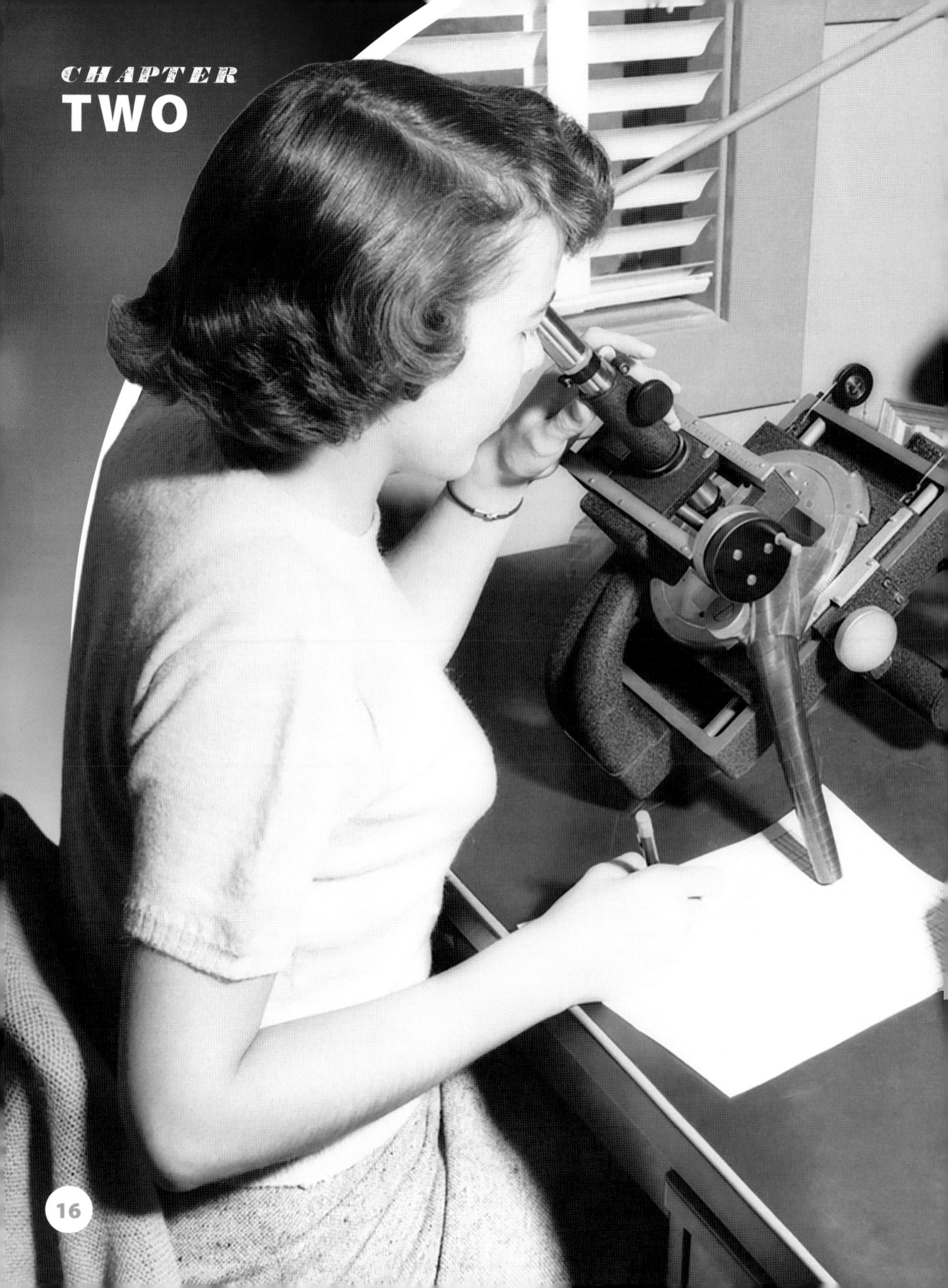

THE PATH TO NASA

Electronic computers are relatively new. People invented them in the mid-1900s. Until that time, humans did all the computing. People who were skilled at math did the calculations electronic computers do today.

Human computing began in 1705 with the discovery of Halley's Comet. Edmond Halley was an English astronomer and mathematician. He wanted to determine the comet's path around the Sun. He could not work out the equations he needed, but French astronomer Alexis-Claude Clairaut did in 1758. Clairaut did not complete the work alone. Astronomers

Human computers used special equipment to help them make calculations.

Human computers helped track the path of Halley's comet around the Sun.

Joseph-Jérôme Lalande and Nicole-Reine Lepaute, a woman, helped. The trio worked for many months and succeeded where Halley did not.

Doing complicated math could take hours and hours. For scientists such as Clairaut, having someone else do that math saved him time. But few scientists were wealthy enough to hire a mathematician.

Human computers later began doing work with navigation. Ship captains used the sky as a map. Stars and planets were guides. Human computers used math to figure out the movements of the objects in the sky. In the 1800s, the British Royal Navy relied on men to do this math. These men worked long hours. Their work included making sure chronometers were accurate. Chronometers were instruments that helped captains navigate by keeping very accurate time.

In the mid-1800s, some human computers in the United States formed a group to do similar work. They published the *Nautical Almanac*, a book for ship captains. It gave the locations of planets and stars. Members of the group did their work by hand. But mechanical machines soon became available to help with calculations. One popular machine was powered by a crank on its side. Another calculating machine was called a Comptometer. It was the size of a large book and had rows of buttons labeled 0 through 9. But these machines were expensive. Few people could afford them. Businesses bought these machines, and human computers began to work in offices. Insurance companies hired human computers. They needed people with math skills.

In the late 1800s, women in the United States began working as computers. After the American Civil War (1861–1865), positions became available to women because many young men had died in the war. Within only a few decades, most computers were women. That is because companies could pay women less than men.

During World War I (1914–1918), many women human computers did military work. They determined bomb trajectories and wind resistance on airplanes. Several of these women worked for the US Army at the Aberdeen Proving Ground in Maryland. Others worked for the US government at the National Advisory Committee for Aeronautics (NACA). This agency would later become NASA.

NACA

The US government created NACA in 1915. Other countries had better airplane technology than the United States. The US government wanted to catch up. At first the plan for NACA did not include research.

A 1913 ad promotes the Comptometer, a calculating machine that human computers used.

But in 1920, NACA opened Langley Aeronautical Laboratory in Virginia. Langley was NACA's first testing site. The number of people who worked at Langley grew quickly, jumping from 15 in 1920 to more than 100 in 1925.

In NACA's early years, Langley workers tested model and full-size aircraft. The tests were usually done in wind tunnels NACA built. During the 1930s and 1940s, NACA continued to grow. NACA created two additional testing sites.

In the 1940s, millions of jobs were available in the defense industry because of World War II. Many black people moved to cities where these jobs were available. They hoped they would find good job opportunities. But

LANGLEY'S COMPUTERS

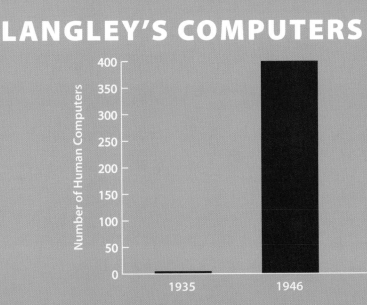

During the 1940s, the number of human computers at Langley grew dramatically. The above graph shows the number of human computers at Langley in 1935 and later in 1946. What caused the increase? How were human computers important at Langley?

many people would not hire African Americans because of their skin color.

In 1941 President Franklin Roosevelt made it illegal for the defense industry to discriminate against employees. By 1943 NACA had hired African American women computers. They worked at Langley. NACA recruited the women from black colleges across the country. The United States needed aircraft to fight in World War II. Advancing aircraft technology

GETTING HIRED

The women mathematicians at NACA learned about job openings in different ways. NACA sent brochures and recruiters to school campuses. NACA sometimes placed ads in journals or newspapers, such as the *Norfolk Journal and Guide*. This newspaper's readers were African Americans who lived in Virginia. Some applicants heard about Langley from family, fellow students, or friends. All applicants had to pass a civil service exam. The exam typically measured math or verbal skills. Black applicants had an additional requirement. These women had to pass a chemistry class at Hampton Institute in Virginia. This included women who already had a degree in chemistry.

was important. Planes needed to fly farther and faster while using less fuel. NACA needed the skills of computers for aircraft and bombing calculations.

In the 1950s, NACA's focus shifted. The United States and the Soviet Union each began to develop new weapons and technologies. The threat of an actual war was very real. The US government wanted to be prepared if the Soviet Union attacked.

NACA researchers worked on missile warheads. These weapons could go into outer space and then return to Earth's atmosphere to hit targets.

NACA also began to think about sending a man into space in the 1950s. But that would not happen under NACA. A historic event in 1957 forever changed the world and the agency.

FURTHER EVIDENCE

Chapter Two has a lot of information about the history of human computers and NACA. What is one of the main points of this chapter? What key evidence supports this point? Go to the article about women at Langley at the website below. Find a quote from the website that supports this main point.

FROM COMPUTERS TO LEADERS: WOMEN AT NASA LANGLEY
abdocorelibrary.com/hidden-heroes

CHAPTER THREE

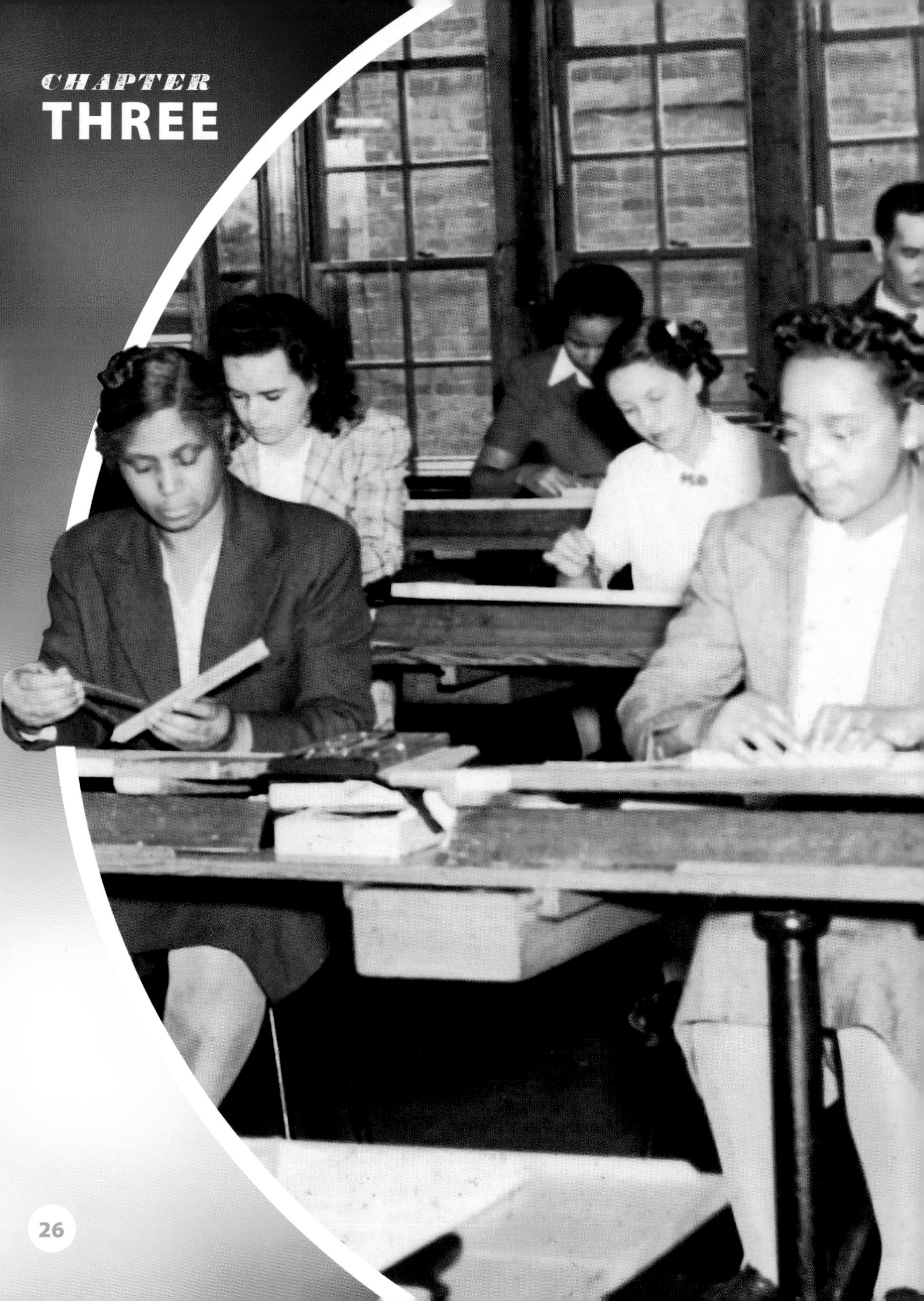

WORKING AT NASA

On October 4, 1957, the Soviet Union launched *Sputnik*. It was the first satellite to be launched into space. The United States rushed to meet the challenge. In 1958 the US government changed NACA's focus and its name. The agency was renamed the National Aeronautics and Space Administration (NASA). Its focus would be developing spacecraft. The United States wanted to beat the Soviet Union in the space race. Meanwhile, African American computers fought challenges of their own.

African American women had to pass a class at Hampton Institute in Virginia before they could become computers at NACA.

JIM CROW LAWS

In the late 1800s, southern states created Jim Crow laws. The name "Jim Crow" came from the name of a character played by a white actor in the early 1800s. The actor painted his face black and pretended to be a clumsy and unintelligent black slave. Jim Crow laws segregated black and white people in public places, including schools and businesses. The facilities and services provided to black people were often worse than those provided to white people. Breaking a Jim Crow law could result in a fine and jail time.

DISCRIMINATION

During World War I, NACA's human computers were all white women. Segregation laws kept black and white people separate in workplaces and other public spaces. Many employers, including NACA, did not hire African Americans.

Black women began working as computers for NACA in great numbers after Roosevelt desegregated the defense industry. Several NACA employees became

Jeanette Scissum worked as a human computer at Marshall Space Flight Center in Huntsville, Alabama.

"COLORED" SIGNS

Miriam Daniel Mann worked at Langley for NACA and NASA. Mann was born in Georgia in 1907. She got a degree in chemistry from Alabama's Talladega College. She also studied math. Langley hired Mann as a computer in 1943. She worked in the wind tunnels and on the spacecraft John Glenn rode in when he orbited Earth. Mann's daughter, Miriam Mann Harris, talked about the discrimination Mann and other black computers faced at Langley: "She would relate stories about the 'colored' sign on a table in the back of the cafeteria. She brought the first one home, but there was a replacement the next day. New signs went up on the bathroom door, 'colored girls.'"

NASA employees after the agency's name changed in 1957. Katherine Johnson, Mary Jackson, Annie Easley, and other African American computers were among them.

At Langley the black women mathematicians worked in a separate area called West Area Computing. They were known as the West Area Computers. These women did the same work as their white coworkers.

But they were treated differently. They had to use a separate bathroom. They had to sit at a table in the cafeteria designated for them.

Miriam Daniel Mann was one of NACA's first black human computers. She worked at Langley for 23 years. She fought against segregation. She removed segregation signs from the cafeteria and the bathroom door.

African American women computers were also discriminated against because they were women. They earned less for doing the same work as male junior engineers. These men earned $2,600 per year. The women, regardless of race, earned just $1,440 per year as junior computers. Still, many of the women were happy to have their jobs. They were paid more than they would have been in most other jobs that were available to them. Some of the computers had been teachers. At the time, a teacher's salary was approximately $550 per year. The women also got to

Human computer Christine Darden worked in NASA's wind tunnels.

use their mathematics degrees. Job opportunities for women were limited. NASA gave women options other than teaching.

The African American women who worked at NASA did not let any challenges get the best of them. They used their skills. They met the demands of the job. Their work helped create an amazing space program and pave the way for other black women.

STRAIGHT TO THE
SOURCE

In a 2001 interview, Annie Easley described a time when she experienced discrimination in the workplace:

We had a piece of equipment. . . . There were six people that worked on it, and someone took a picture of us in a work situation. . . . They blew it up to put it on display. I was cut out of that picture. I was so embarrassed. . . . I said something to my room supervisor. She says, "Oh, I don't blame you. I'd be upset, too." And that was the end of it.

But my thing is, if I can't work with you, I will work around you. I was not about to be so discouraged that I'd walk away. That may be a solution for some people, but it's not mine.

Source: Sandra Johnson. "NASA Headquarters Oral History Project: Edited Oral History Transcript." *NASA*. National Aeronautics and Space Administration, July 16, 2010. Web. Accessed May 1, 2018.

What's the Big Idea?

Take a close look at this passage. What point is Easley making about what it was like to be a woman of color at her workplace? How did she respond to discrimination?

CHAPTER
FOUR

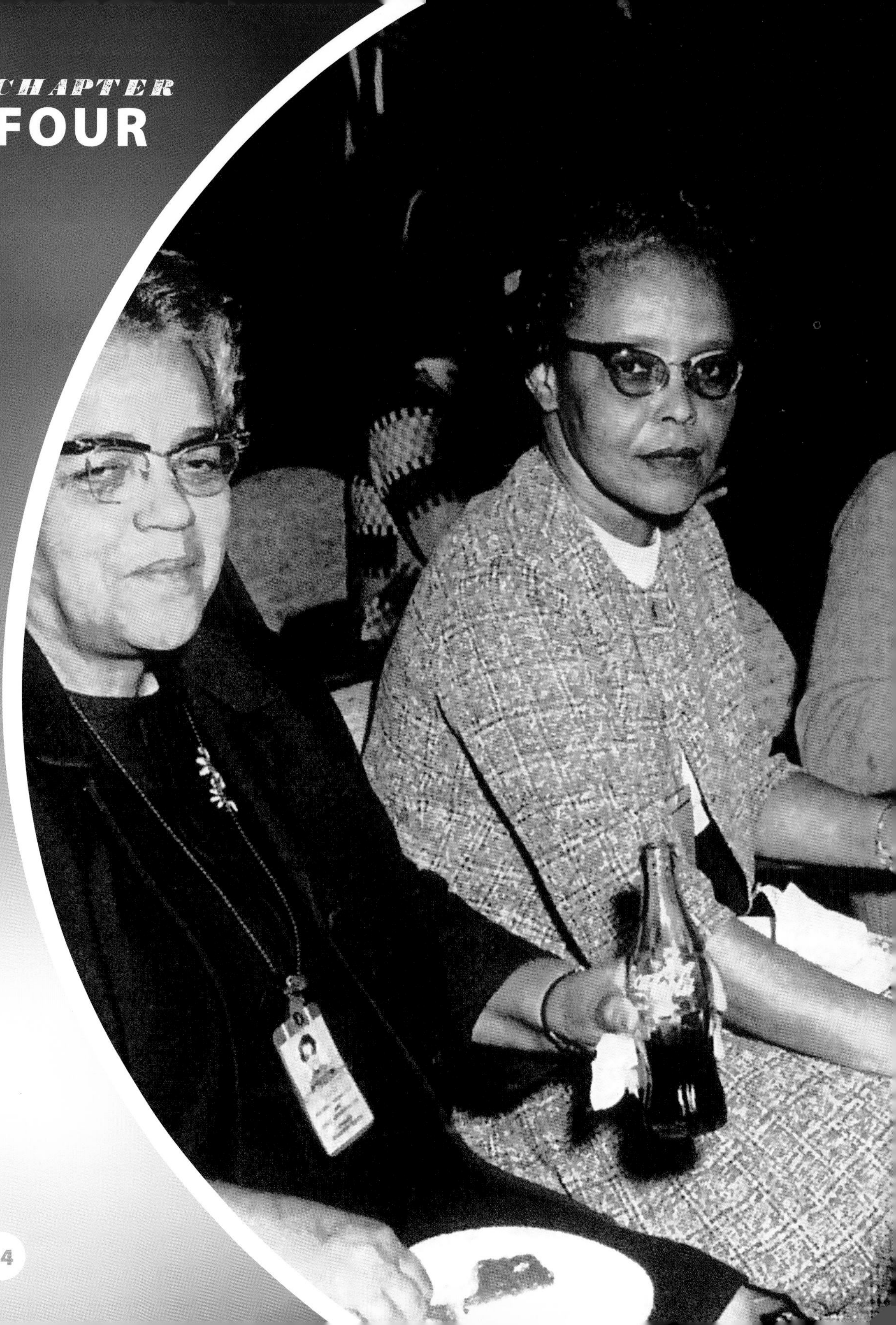

TRAILBLAZERS

The West Area Computers became role models. This was true at NACA and beyond. Dorothy Vaughan was one of the first computers at Langley. Vaughan started working at NACA in 1943. In 1949 the agency put her in charge of the West Area Computers. She was NACA's first black supervisor. She held the role until the West Area Computing office closed in 1958.

Vaughan also led in another way. When NASA adopted electronic computers in the early 1960s, the organization no longer needed human computers. But Vaughan and her fellow computers did not leave. Instead they learned computer skills. They studied FORTRAN, a

NASA employees, including human computer Dorothy Vaughan, *left*, pose for a photo in 1950.

Mary Jackson was the first African American woman engineer hired at NASA.

computer programming language. After becoming experts at FORTRAN, the women taught the engineers how to use it.

During her time at NASA, Mary Jackson also changed jobs. NACA hired her as a computer in 1951. In 1958 she began working as an engineer. In 1979 Jackson became a manager. She led the affirmative action program and the women's program at Langley. These programs promoted equality and supported the needs of NASA's women employees. As a manager, Jackson encouraged NASA to promote and employ women.

Annie Easley's role changed over time too. Easley worked at Langley from 1955 to 1989. She became an expert in FORTRAN. She wrote the code for a rocket. Her code was the groundwork for many NASA launches, including satellites and space shuttles. She later created batteries for electric vehicles, including Mars rovers. The Mars rovers are vehicles that explore the planet Mars.

BUILDING ON THEIR WORK

HONORING KATHERINE JOHNSON

On November 24, 2015, President Barack Obama gave Johnson the Presidential Medal of Freedom. This is the highest honor a nonmilitary person can receive in the United States. Two years later, a new building called the Katherine Johnson Computational Research Facility opened at Langley. The 99-year-old former human computer was surprised when she found out NASA was naming the building after her. The building is dedicated to a variety of research, including modeling and data analysis.

Other black women have built on the work of NASA's human computers. In the late 1960s, Nichelle Nichols played Lieutenant Uhura on *Star Trek*. Her small part had a big effect on many viewers. She was the first standout African American character on television. Uhura was not simply in the background. Viewers knew she was a strong, important character.

NASA saw potential in Nichols. The agency asked her to recruit people to work for NASA. Nichols began doing that work in the 1970s. She visited universities and talked to science and engineering students about working for NASA.

Nichols's appearance on *Star Trek* influenced African American astronaut Mae Jemison. Jemison became NASA's first African American woman astronaut in 1987. In September 1992, she became the first African American woman in space. Since then, four other African American women have been NASA astronauts.

TELLING THEIR STORY

The human computers were known at Langley. But many Americans did not know about these women, especially those who worked in West Area Computing. They were hidden from history until other women began to tell their stories.

In the 1990s, historian Beverly Golemba talked to 13 women who had worked as computers at Langley. She wrote a paper based on her research called "Human Computers: The Women in Aeronautical Research." Golemba did not publish her paper, so few people knew about it.

Author Margot Lee Shetterly's work

HUMAN COMPUTERS TIMELINE

1914
World War I began. Many white women began to work for the US military as computers.

1935
Five women began working as the first computers at NACA's Langley testing site.

1949
Dorothy Vaughan became NACA's first black supervisor.

1962
John Glenn became the first American to orbit Earth.

2016
Margot Lee Shetterly's book about NASA's black computers, *Hidden Figures*, was published.

1915
The US Congress founded NACA.

1941
Franklin Roosevelt made discrimination in the defense industry illegal.

1958
NACA became NASA and changed its focus to space flight.

2015
President Barack Obama gave Katherine Johnson the Presidential Medal of Freedom.

The above timeline shows key events relating to the history of human computers at NACA and NASA. How did human computers shape NACA and NASA? How might this timeline be different if NACA and NASA hadn't hired human computers?

on NASA's human computers has gotten much more attention. She wrote the book *Hidden Figures: The American Dream and the Untold Story of the Black Women Mathematicians Who Helped Win the Space Race*. In the book, Shetterly focuses on five of the black women computers. The movie *Hidden Figures* came out in 2016. It is based on Shetterly's work. It features the stories of Jackson, Johnson, and Vaughan.

In 2019 the story of NASA's human computers was turned into a play. The play premiered in Hopkins, Minnesota. It explores the legacy of these women.

Today, NASA's website has biographies and other articles about human computers. Macalester College in Saint Paul, Minnesota, has a developed an online database about these women.

The women of West Area Computing are no longer hidden. Their stories and work have been in the spotlight. Now they can inspire more people than ever before.

EXPLORE ONLINE

Chapter Four talks about the legacy of NASA's human computers. The website below goes into more depth on this topic. As you know, every source is different. How is the information given on the website different from the information in this chapter? What new information did you learn from this website?

HUMAN COMPUTERS: THE WOMEN OF NASA
abdocorelibrary.com/hidden-heroes

FAST FACTS

- White women began working as human computers for NACA during World War I.

- NACA started hiring black women as computers during World War II. The black women were segregated into their own group called West Area Computing.

- Human computers first helped NACA with calculations for the development of weapons.

- In 1958 NACA became NASA. It changed its focus to spacecraft development and space exploration. Human computers did math for space flight and re-entry.

- Several African American computers helped with NASA astronaut John Glenn's 1962 mission to orbit Earth, including Katherine Johnson.

- Electronic computers replaced human computers at NASA in the 1960s. But the women continued to help NASA by becoming programmers.

- In 2016 Margot Lee Shetterly's book *Hidden Figures* brought attention to NASA's human computers. It inspired the film of the same name.

STOP AND
THINK

You Are There

Chapter One talks about how NASA's human computers supported John Glenn's 1962 mission. Imagine you were a human computer at NASA helping with this mission. Write a letter home telling your friends about your experience. Be sure to add plenty of details.

Say What?

Studying the history of NASA's human computers can mean learning a lot of new vocabulary. Find five words in this book that you've never heard before. Use a dictionary to find out what they mean. Then write the meanings in your own words, and use each word in a sentence.

Surprise Me

Chapter Four discusses the legacy of NASA's human computers. After reading this book, what two or three facts about their legacy did you find most surprising? Write a few sentences about each fact. Why did you find each fact surprising?

GLOSSARY

capsule
a small part of a spacecraft where an astronaut lives and works while in space

catwalks
raised platforms that workers use to reach machines

code
a language that is made up of symbols, such as letters and numbers, that a computer can read

cosmonaut
an astronaut from the Soviet Union

discriminate
to mistreat a person or group based on race or other perceived differences

orbit
to travel around something, such as a planet

recruit
to search for people to work at a business or to join a group or the military

satellite
an object that circles another object that is bigger

segregation
the separation of people of different races or ethnic groups through separate schools and other public spaces

ONLINE RESOURCES

To learn more about NASA's human computers, visit our free resource websites below.

Visit **abdocorelibrary.com** for free Common Core resources for teachers and students, including vetted activities, multimedia, and booklinks, for deeper subject comprehension.

Visit **abdobooklinks.com** for free additional online weblinks for further learning. These links are routinely monitored and updated to provide the most current information available.

LEARN MORE

Edwards, Sue Bradford, and Duchess Harris, JD, PhD. *Hidden Human Computers*. Minneapolis, MN: Abdo Publishing, 2017.

Gagne, Tammy. *Women in Earth and Space Exploration*. Minneapolis, MN: Abdo Publishing, 2017.

ABOUT THE
AUTHORS

Duchess Harris, JD, PhD

Professor Harris is the chair of the American Studies department at Macalester College and curator of the Duchess Harris Collection of ABDO books. She is the author and coauthor of recently released ABDO books including *Hidden Human Computers: The Black Women of NASA, Black Lives Matter,* and *Race and Policing.*

Before working with ABDO, she authored several other books on the topics of race, culture, and American history. She served as an associate editor for *Litigation News,* the American Bar Association Section of Litigation's quarterly flagship publication, and was the first editor in chief of *Law Raza,* an interactive online journal covering race and the law, published at William Mitchell College of Law. She has earned a PhD in American Studies from the University of Minnesota and a JD from William Mitchell College of Law.

Rebecca Rowell

Rebecca Rowell has put her degree in publishing and writing to work as an editor and an author of many books. Her recent books include *Emmanuel Macron: President of France* and *The American Middle Class* (cowritten with Duchess Harris). She lives in Minneapolis, Minnesota.

INDEX

astronomers, 17–19

computer programming, 35–37

Easley, Annie, 30, 33, 36–37

Glenn, John, 7, 9, 11–12, 14, 30

Hidden Figures, 15, 40
human computers, 10–11, 17–20, 28–32, 35, 39

Jackson, Mary, 22, 30, 36, 40
Jemison, Mae, 38
Jim Crow laws, 28
Johnson, Katherine, 8–12, 14, 15, 30, 37, 40

Langley testing site, 15, 21–23, 24, 30–31, 35, 36, 37, 38–39

Mann, Miriam Daniel, 30, 31

NACA, 15, 20–25, 27, 28, 30, 31, 35, 36
NASA, 7, 9–11, 12, 14, 15, 17, 20, 22, 27, 30, 32, 35, 36, 37, 38, 41
Nichols, Nichelle, 37–38

Obama, Barack, 37

Presidential Medal of Freedom, 37

Roosevelt, Franklin, 23, 28

segregation, 28, 30–31
Shetterly, Margot Lee, 15, 39–40
ship navigation, 19
Soviet Union, 8, 9, 24–25, 27

Vaughan, Dorothy, 35, 40

West Area Computers, 30, 35, 38, 41
wind tunnels, 22, 30
World War II, 8, 23–24